DON'T FLOSS YOUR TOES

PHOTOGRAPHY BY TRISH GLAB PHOTOGRAPHY (www.trishglabphotography.com)

Library and Archives Canada Cataloguing in Publication
Townsin, Felix, author
Don't floss your toes : advice from a 5 year old / Felix Townsin.
ISBN 978-1-928131-08-3 (hardback)
1. Children--Quotations. 2. Conduct of life--Quotations, maxims, etc. I. Title.
PN6328.C5T68 2017 305.233 C2016-905785-2

PEOPLE WILL STILL LIKE YOU IF YOUR SOCKS DON'T MATCH.

DON'T CLIMB ROTTEN TREES.

GIVE YOUR GRANDPARENTS LOTS OF HUGS.

DON'T GO NEAR A VOLCANO WHEN YOU HEAR IT RUMBLING.

IT'S ALWAYS A GOOD TIME TO WEAR A FANCY HAT.

DON'T LICK YOUR FINGERS - UNLESS THEY ARE COVERED IN CHOCOLATE.

PEEL YOUR BANANAS FROM THE BOTTOM UP.

TOYS AND TEDDIES CAN BE REPLACED, BUT FRIENDS AND FAMILY CANNOT.

SOMETIMES IT'S JUST GOOD TO BE REALLY CRAZY

WE HAVE HEARTS FOR LOVING AND FOR MAKING BLOOD.

SPOONS CAN BE USED FOR ANYTHING - A SHOVEL, A KNIFE, A SWORD, AN EYE PATCH.

TAKE PICTURES - ESPECIALLY IF YOU DON'T HAVE A GOOD MEMORY.

TRY AND FIND THE POT OF GOLD AT THE END OF A RAINBOW. IT MIGHT NOT BE THERE BECAUSE SIMON SAID HE FOUND IT ALREADY AND BURIED IT.

YOU CAN FIND LOVE BY FILLING SOMEONE'S BUCKET.

MAKE YOUR OWN ART.

DON'T BE AFRAID OF THE DOCTOR. IT IS MOSTLY NURSES WHO GIVE YOU NEEDLES.

IF YOUR PANTS ARE TOO TIGHT TO PUT ON, UNZIP THE ZIPPER.

DON'T BUY THINGS THAT ARE SUPER EXPENSIVE UNLESS YOU HAVE MORE THAN THAT MUCH MONEY.

CHOCOLATE IS NOT GOOD FOR YOU, BUT YOU SHOULD TRY IT.

DON'T TRY AND OPEN WALNUTS WITH YOUR BARE HANDS.

DADS SHOULDN'T SAY SHHHH SO LOUD.

DO NOT LOOK BACK.

RIDE A PONY INSTEAD OF A HORSE - THEY ARE SMALLER, SLOWER AND BEAUTIFULER.

IF YOU HAVE A MAP YOU CAN COPY THE MAP ONTO A PIECE OF PAPER - THEN YOU WILL HAVE TWO MAPS!

IF YOU LIKE CATS, GO TO THAILAND, THERE ARE LOTS OF THEM.

IF YOU GO TO SPACE, MAKE SURE TO UNBUCKLE YOUR SEATBELT - YOU WILL FLOAT.

DON'T BOTHER CATS.

EAT YOUR TOAST UPSIDE DOWN - THE TOPPINGS TASTE BETTER WHEN THEY TOUCH YOUR TONGUE. PIZZA TOO.

YOU SHOULD FIND YOUR FAVOURITE JOB THAT YOU WANTED TO BE WHEN YOU WERE LITTLE.

DON'T CHOP DOWN ALL THE TREES OR YOU WON'T HAVE ANY AIR.

WATCH OUT FOR MOSQUITOES - THEY HAVE LONG NOSES TO SUCK UP YOUR BLOOD!

IF YOU LOVE YOUR MOTHER DON'T DO BAD THINGS TO HER.

WALK, JUMP, SWING.

LOVE IS THE BEST PRESENT YOU CAN GET.

EVEN THOUGH SOME BOYS THINK PINK IS A GIRL COLOUR, IT REALLY ISN'T. SOME BOYS LIKE IT, JUST LIKE MY DAD... AND ME.

ALWAYS BE READY FOR WINTER.

WHEN THERE IS SOMETHING SCARY, DON'T PANIC. I DON'T REALLY KNOW WHY, I JUST HEARD UNCLE DARRYL SAY THAT.

IF SOMEONE TRIES TO SQUISH YOU - RUN!

ALWAYS KEEP YOUR WINDSCREEN CLEAN.

ORIGAMI IS SO RELAXING, IF YOU DO THE RIGHT TYPE. THE OTHER TYPE GETS YOU REALLY FRUSTRATED.

DON'T KNOCK DOWN A COCOON. THE BUTTERFLY WILL HAVE A CROOKED WING AND DIE.

IF YOU ARE COLD SNUGGLE UP WITH SOMEONE.

DON'T PUNCH - UNLESS YOU HAVE BOXING GLOVES ON AND YOU ARE IN A BOXING RING.

USE PAPER TOWEL TO OPEN DOORS IN PUBLIC BATHROOMS. YOU DON'T NEED TO DO THIS IN YOUR OWN BATHROOM.

WHEN YOU MAKE A PASSWORD CHOOSE SOMETHING YOU CAN REMEMBER.

YOU MUST TRY LASAGNE. I LOVE IT.

IF YOU HAVE FISH OIL, I NEED TO WARN YOU - IT TASTES LIKE NOTHING, BUT WITH A NOT VERY NICE FLAVOUR IN IT.

BE QUIET WHEN BABIES ARE SLEEPING.

IF YOU LIKE VIDEO GAMES GO ON A CRUISE SHIP.

EAT SUSHI SOMETIMES - IT IS REALLY GOOD.

DON'T LET YOUR FEET TAKE A NAP. IT MAKES THEM FEEL BUZZY, LIKE THEY HAVE LIGHTENING IN THEM.

IF YOU ARE IN TROUBLE CALL A SUPERHERO.

YOU SHOULD BUY A DREAM CATCHER IF YOU HAVE BAD DREAMS A LOT.

IF YOU LOVE SOMEONE DRAW LOVEHEARTS ON THEIR BIRTHDAY CARD.

PICK UP GIANT CRABS AT THE BACK OF THEIR BACK. PICK UP LITTLE CRABS WHEREVER YOU WANT.

DON'T RUN WITH FLIP FLOPS - YOU MIGHT TRIP.

MAKE A SNOWMAN.

THE BEST THING TO DO WITH GINGER IS TO MAKE A GINGERBREAD HOUSE.

DON'T POLLUTE THE PLANET.

MISO SOUP IS DELICIOUS ON SUNNY DAYS, OR ANY DAY.

SMELL FLOWERS.

BUCKLE UP - WHAT DO YOU WANT TO DO GO TO JAIL OR BUCKLE UP?

BE CAREFUL OF MONSTERS.

YOU SHOULD LOVE A GRANDPA.

THERE IS NOTHING MORE RELAXING THAN A LITTLE SUNBATHING.

ADVICE TO PARENTS - DON'T GET SO MAD.

FIND WORMS - THEY ARE GREAT FOR YOUR GARDEN. THEY MAKE DIRT BY POOPING OUT SOIL. IT SMELLS LIKE SOIL AND IT IS SOIL.

IF YOU LIKE BEAUTIFUL THINGS GO FIND SOME JEWELS.

YOU SHOULD TRY SNORKELLING, BUT YOU MIGHT GET SO COLD, LIKE EVEN COLDER THAN SNOW. I THINK IT TOOK ME A DAY TO WARM UP.

IT'S NOT ABOUT WINNING, IT'S ABOUT HAVING FUN. YOU SHOULD TRY TO WIN IF YOU LIKE WINNING.

KNOCK ON THE DOOR BEFORE YOU GO IN THE BATHROOM. ONLY GO IN IF THERE IS NO ANSWER.

BE CAREFUL IN A POTATO SACK RACE - YOUR PANTS MIGHT FALL DOWN.

YOU SHOULDN'T HIDE UNDER A TREE IF THERE IS LIGHTENING. THE LIGHTENING USUALLY STRIKES THE TREE AND YOU MIGHT GET ELECTROCUTED. YOU WOULDN'T LIKE THAT, WOULD YOU?

DON'T SWALLOW BUBBLE GUM. I DON'T KNOW WHY. JUST DON'T.

THE BEST PLACE TO LOOK FOR A FAIRY IS THE MAGICAL FOREST.

IF YOU TELL THE TRUTH YOUR PARENTS WILL BE LESS MAD.

IF YOU JUMP IN MUD PUDDLES WEAR YOUR BOOTS.

TAKE A TRIP TO THE BEACH.

MAKE YOUR OWN CHRISTMAS PRESENTS.

DON'T EAT YOUR HAIR - YOU WILL GET A HAIR BALL.

GRANDMAS ARE GOOD FOR LOVING AND HUGGING.
GRANDMAS ARE NOT GOOD FOR BUGGING.

THE BEST WAY TO EAT KALE IS KALE CHIPS.

IF YOU WANT TO DANCE REALLY GOOD WATCH MUSIC VIDEOS.

THE BEST WAY TO CLEAN UP IS TO MAKE A GAME OF IT.

ANTS CAN BITE, EVEN THOUGH THEY ARE TINY!

IF YOU HAVE TO GET A NEEDLE, YOUR MOM AND DAD SHOULD LET YOU HAVE A CELEBRATION AFTER.

DON'T BREATHE THROUGH YOUR NOSE WHEN THERE IS SOMETHING STINKY.

NEVER LEAVE BOOKS THAT YOU LOVE BEHIND.

IF YOU HAVE A WASP NEST, DON'T TEASE THEM TOO MUCH. YOU MIGHT GET STUNG ON THE NECK LIKE ME.

DON'T CLIMB ON TREES WITH SKINNY BRANCHES.

BE CAREFUL OF YOUR SANDALS WHEN YOU GO TO SAMOA - THE CRABS MIGHT TAKE THEM. I THINK THE CRABS GET TIRED OF PEOPLE PICKING THEM UP, OR MAYBE THEY ARE TRYING TO MAKE A SANDAL COLLECTION.

ALWAYS LOOK AT THE GROUND IN PLACES THAT HAVE SNAKES.

BLOW A RASPBERRY ON SOMEONE.

IF YOU GO TO JAPAN AND YOU WANTED TO GO TO TOKYO. NO PROBLEM! TOKYO IS IN JAPAN!

NEVER GIVE UP. JUST KEEP TRYING.

DON'T CLIMB ON THINGS THAT HAVE FENCES AROUND THEM.

IF YOU HEAR A SOUND LIKE DALALALALALALALA, THAT MEANS THERE IS A WOODPECKER NEARBY.

WHEN YOU GO TO WORK AND YOU WANT TO LOOK COOL, WEAR SUNGLASSES.

SMILE.

LET DOLPHINS SWIM FREE. YOU SHOULDN'T CAPTURE DOLPHINS AND PUT THEM IN AN AQUARIUM.

DON'T FLOSS YOUR TOES BEFORE YOU FLOSS YOUR TEETH.

DON'T OPEN UMBRELLAS IN THE HOUSE - IT MIGHT HIT EVERYTHING.

SOMETIMES YOU HAVE TO MAKE RULES.

GO ON A ROAD TRIP - DON'T FORGET TO PACK YOUR FAVOURITE BOOK.

YOU MIGHT WANT TO KEEP YOUR LEGO AWAY FROM LITTLE SISTERS - THEY COULD SWALLOW THE PIECES OR THEY MIGHT WRECK YOUR CREATIONS.

MAKE UP YOUR OWN RECIPES.

YOU SHOULD GET 10 HUGS EVERY DAY.

FAIRIES ARE NICE, BUT SHY. YOU SHOULD LOOK FOR THEM, BUT DON'T TRY TO CATCH THEM.

TRY A NEW FOOD.

FESTIVALS ARE REALLY FUN - GO TO ONE.

BE AWARE OF POO.

PUT BLUEBERRIES OR RASPBERRIES IN YOUR WATER. IT TASTES BETTER.

IF YOU ARE GOING ON AN AIRPLANE, MAKE SURE TO TAKE THE RIGHT TYPE - SOME OF THEM HAVE SHOWS AND FOOD ON THEM!

NEVER GO TO THE SUN, UNLESS YOU WEAR SUPER GOOD SUNGLASSES AND A SUPER GOOD SUN SUIT.

IF YOU ARE SLEEPING AND YOU HEAR NOISY BIRDS THAT MEANS IT IS TIME TO WAKE UP.

WHEN SOMEONE YOU LOVE DIES, IT'S PRETTY HARD, BUT YOU NEED TO LIVE YOUR LIFE AGAIN.

PUT TOO MUCH SOAP IN YOUR BUBBLE BATH, YOU WILL GET SO MANY BUBBLES. ONE TIME I HAD SO MANY THEY WENT OVER MY HEAD AND SPILLED ONTO THE FLOOR. I WAS SO SAD TO SEE THAT BATH GO AWAY.

BE KIND.

DON'T CLIMB UP BUILDINGS, UNLESS YOU ARE INSIDE.

WASH YOUR HANDS A LOT.

IF YOU GET CHICKEN BONES, YOU SHOULD MAKE CHICKEN SOUP. IT IS REALLY HEALTHY FOR YOU.

DON'T PUT YOUR HAIR NEAR A GOAT, OR YOUR CLOTHES. HE WILL EAT THEM ALL.

IF YOU FIND A SPIDER IN YOUR HOUSE, SAY HELLO TO IT.

DON'T PULL GRASS BY THE ROOTS UNLESS YOU DON'T WANT IT TO GROW BACK.

IF YOU HAVE A BABY, MAKE SURE YOU ARE READY TO HEAR HER CRY.

TELL YOUR SISTER YOU LOVE HER.

THE EASIEST WAY TO MAKE A GINGERBREAD HOUSE IS TO BUY ONE OF THOSE BOXES FROM THE STORE.

LADY BUGS ARE CUTE. YOU SHOULD TRY TO FIND ONE.

IF YOU ARE HOT TRY AND GET COLD AGAIN.

EAT CABBAGE.

RAINY DAYS ARE BEST FOR HOUSE FIRES.

STRAWBERRIES STAIN. EAT THEM OVER A PLATE.

WHEN YOU GET OLD YOU GET CRINKLY SKIN.YOU SHOULD BEWARE OF YOUR GRANDSON LAUGHING AT YOU. CRINKLY SKIN IS FINE. JUST IGNORE HIM.

CATS MAKE A BETTER PET THAN DOGS - THEY ARE NICE AND DON'T GET QUITE AS EXCITED.

NEIGHBOURS CAN BE ANNOYING.

YOU SHOULD ONLY PICK RIPE FRUIT.

NEVER HURT OLD PEOPLE.

IF YOU BURP AND YOU MEAN TO DO IT, THAT IS VERY RUDE. IF YOU DON'T MEAN TO BURP, BUT YOU FORGET TO SAY EXCUSE ME, THAT IS STILL RUDE.

IF YOU LIKE GOLD GO TO A MINE, OR A CAVE.

EAT HEALTHY FOOD. IT DOESN'T TASTE AS GOOD, BUT IT MAKES YOU STRONG AND IT MAKES YOU GROW.

DON'T GO IN LONG GRASS TOO MUCH, THERE MIGHT BE TICKS THERE.

ALWAYS LOOK OUT FOR FALLING LEAVES - ACTUALLY FALLING LEAVES ARE PRETTY FUN.

A WEDDING IS A REALLY SPECIAL THING. NOW YOU HAVE A WIFE AND YOU DIDN'T BEFORE, OR MAYBE YOU DID AND YOU JUST GOT TO CHANGE WIVES.

NEVER GO NEAR A DINOSAUR. IF YOU SEE ONE RUN AWAY.

IF YOU ARE DOING A HARD PUZZLE, START WITH THE FRAME AND WORK INSIDE UNTIL YOU GET TO THE LAST PIECE.

REMEMBER YOUR PLEASE AND THANK YOUS.

IF YOU HAVE GREY HAIR DON'T PULL IT OUT. IT WON'T MAKE YOU YOUNG.

YOU SHOULDN'T WORRY. YOU MIGHT GET AN ULCER.

IF YOU WANT A GOOD BED GO TO SLEEP COUNTRY. THEY HAVE ALL SORTS OF GOOD BEDS.

YOU SHOULD ALWAYS BE DIFFERENT BECAUSE DOING EVERYTHING THE SAME IS BORING.

IF YOU SLEEP IN A TENT DON'T OPEN THE DOOR. BUGS WILL GET IN, LIKE EARWIGS AND DADDY LONGLEGS. I LIKE DADDY LONGLEGS, BUT NOT EARWIGS.

RECYCLE TO MAKE NEW THINGS.

IF YOU GO TO SPACE YOU SHOULD EXPLORE A PLANET.

TRY TO GROW YOUR OWN FOOD.

READ A NEWSPAPER TO FIND OUT SOME AWESOME NEWS - THAT IS, IF YOU PICK THE RIGHT ONE. IF YOU PICK THE WRONG ONE YOU WILL BE VERY BORED.

YOU SHOULD TRY WET CINNAMON - IT TASTES LIKE CHOCOLATE. IT REALLY DOES!

IF ANYONE KNOWS HOW A BELLY BUTTON TURNS SKIN COLOUR, TELL ME!

BE NICE TO PEOPLE. THEY MAKE GOOD COMPANY.

YOU SHOULDN'T HAVE ELEVEN KIDS. IT IS VERY HARD TO HANDLE THEM.

ASK FOR HELP INSTEAD OF HURTING SOMEONE.

STAY BACK FROM LIONS. THEY BITE.

ASK YOUR MOM FOR AN UNDERDUCK.

IF YOU ARE FRUSTRATED, BREATHE IN THROUGH YOUR NOSE AND OUT THROUGH YOUR MOUTH.

DON'T WALK THROUGH SPIDER WEBS SO YOU WON'T WRECK A SPIDER'S HOME.

IF SOMETHING LOOKS LIKE BUTTER YOU SHOULD TRY IT - IT MIGHT ACTUALLY BE ICING!

IF YOU GO TO GRADE ONE IN FRENCH IMMERSION, THE TEACHER WILL ONLY SPEAK FRENCH TO YOU. IT MIGHT BE HARD ON YOU BECAUSE THEY DON'T TEACH YOU MUCH FRENCH IN KINDERGARTEN.

SWING WHENEVER YOU CAN.

YOU SHOULD FALL ASLEEP AT BEDTIME OR YOU WILL GET CRANKY.

WALK AROUND WITH BARE FEET SOMETIMES, UNLESS YOU ARE ON WOOD CHIPS.

YOU SHOULD TRY APPLE SLICES WITH ALMOND BUTTER - I CALL THEM SWEDISH SWEETS.

BUY YOUR VEGETABLES FROM THE FARM OR A FARMER'S MARKET - THEY HAVE VERY FRESH ONES.

YOU SHOULDN'T LEAVE YOUR FOOD OUTSIDE. FLIES WILL GO ON IT AND THEY WALK ON POO. MY SISTER LEFT HER FOOD AND TWICE A FLY LANDED ON IT.

SISTERS ARE GOOD FOR SNUGGLING.

IF YOU LIKE CUTE THINGS LOOK AT A LITTLE DOG.

DON'T CLIMB A SLIPPERY POLE UNLESS YOU ARE GOING TO WIN A HAM. HAM IS DELICIOUS.

WHEN YOU LOSE YOUR TOOTH, LEAVE THE TOOTH FAIRY A NICE NOTE.

MAYBE TELL YOUR SISTER TO QUIETEN DOWN.

ON HALLOWEEN, WEAR SOMETHING THAT GLOWS ON YOUR BODY.

IF YOU ARE GRUMPY EAT SOMETHING THAT YOU LIKE AND YOU WILL START FEELING HAPPY AGAIN.

THE BOTTOM OF THE HOT CHOCOLATE IS THE BEST!

IF SOMEONE ALWAYS GIVES YOU KISSES AND ALWAYS SMILES AT YOU, IT MEANS THEY LOVE YOU.

TRY TO LOSE YOUR TEETH.

IF YOU SHAVE, PUT SOME SOAP ON FIRST SO YOU DON'T GET CUT. I'M NOT EVEN OLD ENOUGH TO SHAVE AND I KNOW THAT.

VISIT YOUR DENTIST ONCE AND A WHILE. THEY GIVE YOU NEW TOOTHBRUSHES.

DON'T SMELL A SOCK. SOME SOCKS ARE VERY STINKY.

DON'T PICK BLUEBERRIES THAT AREN'T BLUE.

EVEN THOUGH SAUERKRAUT HAS SOUR IN ITS NAME, IT IS NOT SOUR. IT IS VERY SALTY. IT SHOULD BE CALLED SALTYKRAUT.

IF YOU ARE A CANADIAN, AND YOU GO TO AUSTRALIA, IT IS REALLY DIFFERENT. THERE IS MOSTLY FRUITS AND DESSERTS THERE.

EXPERIMENTS ARE A GOOD WAY TO LEARN STUFF ABOUT THE WORLD. SOMETIMES EXPERIMENTS BLOW UP.

YOU SHOULD LOOK INSIDE A HOUSE BEFORE YOU BUY IT.

ONCE IN A LIFETIME YOU SHOULD ROAST YOUR BRUSSEL SPROUTS.

ALWAYS BE READY FOR A TRIP.

IF YOU THINK PEPPER IS REALLY SPICY, IT'S NOT. IT'S REALLY GOOD ON STUFF.

GIRLS LOVE JEWELS. ESPECIALLY JEWELLERY.

RIDE A BIKE WITH TWO WHEELS. IF YOU CAN'T, RIDE A TRICYCLE.

NEVER PULL OUT PLANTS YOU LIKE.

ALWAYS BLOW YOUR NOSE WHEN YOU'VE GOT SNOT IN IT.

IF THERE ARE MOSQUITOES YOU DON'T HAVE TO RUN. JUST CLAP EVERYWHERE AND THAT MIGHT GET THEM AWAY.

IF YOU GET MAD SQUEEZE SOMETHING, BUT NOT A HUMAN.

YOU SHOULD WASH BEHIND YOUR EARS - BROCCOLI COULD GROW THERE, OR ANOTHER PLANT.

MAKE YOUR OWN HAPPY MEAL.

ALWAYS JUMP FAST WHEN YOU ARE IN A SACK.

MAKE SURE TO LOOK AT YOUR GREENS BEFORE YOU EAT THEM. THEY MIGHT HAVE A WORM IN THEM.

WHEN YOU ARE AT SCHOOL YOU SHOULDN'T DO MEAN STUFF NEAR A TEACHER WHO GETS REALLY MAD.

ALWAYS WEAR UNDERWEAR - CLEAN UNDERWEAR.

WATER YOUR PLANTS - THEY LOOK BETTER THAT WAY.

IF SOMEONE IS WEARING A DIAPER AND YOU SMELL SOMETHING, THAT MEANS YOU HAVE TO CHANGE IT.

YOU SHOULD TRY SARDINES, BUT JUST TO WARN YOU, THEY CAN BE VERY SALTY.

DON'T TAKE YOUR BIKE OFF JUMPS IF YOU DON'T KNOW HOW TO CONTROL IT YET.

DON'T GET MAD AT YOUR KIDS WHEN YOU ARE ON A DATE, OR WHEN YOU ARE OUT SOMEWHERE FUN, OR WHEN YOU ARE AT A FRIEND'S HOUSE.

DON'T WASTE TREES, ESPECIALLY ON EARTH DAY.

LEAVE SANTA A BEER AND HE MIGHT LEAVE YOU A BETTER PRESENT.

EAT THE UNHEALTHY TYPE OF PEANUT BUTTER ONCE AND A WHILE - IT TASTES WAY BETTER.

INSTEAD OF BLAMING SOMEONE TELL THE TRUTH.

WHEN YOU GO TO A FARM BE CAREFUL - THERE IS LOTS OF POO AROUND!

DANCE A LOT. IT IS FUN AND HEALTHY.

DO THINGS YOU ARE SCARED OF - IT MIGHT NOT BE AS BAD AS YOU THINK.

JUST WEAR YOUR PYJAMAS SOMETIMES.

YOU SHOULD GET A YOGA MAT WHEN YOU DO YOGA, SO YOU DON'T HURT YOURSELF.

YOU SHOULDN'T PUT SPIKY THINGS NEAR TIRES.

NEVER SHOW YOUR BUM AT SCHOOL.

FEED YOUR GOLDFISH EVERY DAY- IT COULD STOP BREATHING AND DIE.

ALWAYS SING A SONG TO YOURSELF, OR TO THE BIRDS.

IF YOU SEE A GERMAN MONSTER, CLOSE YOUR EYES FOR 10 SECONDS AND THEN OPEN THEM AGAIN AND IT WON'T BE THERE.

IT'S COOL TO MAKE A BOOK.

Felix is five and a half. He loves chocolate, toys, glow-in-the-dark shirts and books. He wants to be a scientist when he grows up, so he can do cool experiments and invent invisibility potions. He has traveled around the world and he loves cats. He eats lots of candies at birthdays and Halloween and the rest of the year he eats soup, broccoli and squash. His wish is to fly. He thinks that if he could fly he might get to school on time. His hope for the future is that people would just be themselves and that scientists will invent something so that people will live forever. He would also like to jump on a cloud and wonders if he would get wet.

My sister Lexi has Blau syndrome. She is the strongest baby. She acts like she doesn't have it and she doesn't cry, even though it hurts so much. She has to get thousands of needles. She likes it when I go with her to the hospital. I hope one of you will help my sister get what she needs and find a cure for Blau syndrome.

-Felix

All the publisher's proceeds from this book have been donated to the CURE BLAU SYNDROME FOUNDATION. Follow Felix, Lexi and family on social media as they journey towards a cure **@memydadandblau.** Learn more about Blau syndrome and its devastating effects and help us make a difference at **www.curebs.com.**